Beyond Standard

Navigating the Standardized Testing Experience

Robert Pimentel & Mateo Pimentel

ISBN-10: 0692205209
ISBN-13: 978-0692205204

DEDICATION

This book is dedicated to my family and especially to my wife, Sheila, who has stood by my side throughout our marriage, always rallying to my support, especially the times that included career changes. Nothing is more exciting and precarious than changing a career path when mortgages, tuitions, food and insurance payments are on the line. I am proud of the loving care Sheila has provided our children throughout their lives. Matthew, Megan and Marcus have a remarkable mother, and I married a remarkable woman who has shared her life and love with me.

CONTENTS

FOREWORD

First and foremost, this book is for parents; its purpose is to share some keen insights about their child's experience with standardized testing. This testing is part of a process that has become integral to the American educational system. Still, so much about it seems to be hidden in plain sight, unfolding only as the process occurs. But rather than offering perfect hindsight, we want to bring vital information into focus for parents who either await the process, or are experiencing it. For this reason and many others, it is our collective hope to help parents understand why standardized testing presents many difficulties for students. Furthermore, because parents are primarily responsible for their child, we believe they can do much to reduce the challenges presented by standardized testing. We hope that by highlighting some of the most prevalent misconceptions, parents can help ensure greater student achievement. We thank you for your interest in our book, a work that we hope will be of value to both you and your student.

INTRODUCTION

Have you ever watched a guitarist pick up an instrument and begin playing without a single sheet of music? Perhaps this occurs only after years of training, coupled with a passion for making music. Perhaps the guitarist is very gifted. Often, musicians are simply drawn to magnificent instruments and elect to learn how to make wonderful music. They can find the results of practice and dedication to be very rewarding. In the same way, some students are drawn to their studies, while others are not. Perhaps, for the first type of student, the dedication to study is simply the fruit of many discipline-filled years. Then again, the student may be very gifted.

The reality is that not all students who experience the standardized testing process are naturally destined for a perfect score. Moreover, to think that intelligence alone will guarantee a great score is to misunderstand what really happens in the testing experience.

Something must also be said for the average

student, who represents the majority of students, and who may need more instruction relative to the benefits of dedicated learning. For many students, it is very easy to lock into a sport, dance, clubs, technology, and a variety of interests that can absorb them. These activities can impact their development in becoming great students.

And while some students have an innate ability to perform well on many levels, there are those—the majority—who can get a bit lost or daunted by the college application process.

Whatever the case may be, the right time to plan for a college career is when the student is knee-deep in sports or clubs. In other words, students should pay attention to their collegiate future sooner, rather than later. Standardized testing is the perfect place to start.

There is a process of study and discipline relative to standardized testing in which training and practice can generate excellent scores. Any student can experience this part of the process and pursue excellence. This is the good news about navigating standardized testing.

Embarking

The college application process is one of the most important aspects of a student's high school career; this very much includes standardized testing. Consider the following: A very small portion of students will achieve top scores, while the majority will score at average levels. In an age of advanced technology, how does this happen? With immediate access to so much information and knowledge, how can so many students earn such average scores? Does this mean a student cannot do better than statistics predict?

The truth is that there are a great many questions that must be addressed to arrive at a well-developed answer. For example, did the student who scored average marks prepare for the test? Did he or she really study? If the student did study, then what was it that he or she studied? *Where* did the student study, and how did the course prepare him or her to be successful? Was it in a large group, a small group, or on an individual basis? Do you, as a parent, or student, know which learning style is most conducive to high scores in your personal situation? While by no means exhaustive, these questions demonstrate how external factors can affect outcomes in standardized testing.

The foregoing questions and many more like them can help us understand a child's experience with standardized testing. Possibly, the overall experience is bigger than the sum of its parts; however, each piece matters when constructing the puzzle so that the complete picture makes as much sense as possible. When unpacking the pieces of the college application process and weighing the impact of standardized testing scores on an application, the situation becomes much more critical and time-sensitive.

It is very important to remember that standardized testing can mean money in addition to college admittance. To actualize this possibility, students must perform at a very high level to compete for thousands of potential scholarship dollars. Who among us is averse to the possibility of receiving free money?

Gauging Conditions

Knowing that a student can take a standardized test for college admittance multiple times should provide even greater insight into the college application process. The testing process was most likely designed for students seeking success. Furthermore, it was probably a safe bet that students might attempt the test several times given the possibility of doing better each time. On the other hand, if the test were administered only once, then maybe a greater number of students would not show up on test day to merely *see how they do*. No potential driver would risk failing the driver's exam just to see how he or she performs without studying. In fact, every driver must review the driver's manual to prepare to pass the test, regardless of the number of times a prospective driver is allowed to test.

When it comes to standardized testing, there is no threat of a one-time-only predicament.

But if it were a one-time-only situation, students might actually study the material first! They might be forced to make an earnest attempt at studying to obtain the highest score possible. Imagine that. Students might study for the exam. Yet, because students are free to test more than once, they endure standardized testing without ever having studied. Why take the test *just to take it?*

What could a haphazard score possibly indicate to the parent or student? Such a score does not necessarily indicate student performance; it is nothing more than a shot in the dark. Ultimately, the common line of thinking embodied in the phrase, "we just want to see how our son or daughter will do," does not harmonize with preparing for the highest score possible. At some level, this is choosing not to put the best foot forward.

Let us be honest about one thing: most parents have taken a test at some point in their lives; they know that preparation generally ensures a better outcome. Students know they have to study for tests in school, so why wouldn't they study for a standardized test? Knowing that preparation is a natural prerequisite for most tests, can we really expect students to excel or perform better than average on standardized testing without providing test training? The answer is no.

Taking the Helm

Do school tests prepare students for standardized tests? In fact, the two areas of study—the liberal arts curriculum and standardized testing—are often confused when answering this question. It is true that bits and pieces of standardized testing material find their way into a general curriculum; nevertheless, thinking that high school students naturally, or by some way of osmosis, receive the skills necessary to succeed on a standardized test is flawed. Because both types of testing are so different, associating them turns out to be nothing more than a common misconception. This is a very good piece of information to know.

Consider English class, one of the cornerstones of a liberal arts curriculum. While standardized testing vocabulary words do show up in an English class, it does not mean that the English class itself will necessarily have a profound bearing on standardized testing's fill-in-the-blank questions. Furthermore, an English class may not explore any context as to the strategic dissection of standardized test questions, *or* how to appropriately employ vocabulary on the test. The truth is that there is no correlation between achieving an A+ in English class and dominating either the writing or the English sections on a standardized test.

It is plain to see that both *how* and *what* a student learns in school does not wholly translate to standardized testing. After all, a high school education has a much more holistic purpose than culminating in standardized testing. Both class and test might make use of the same language, but other than that, there is no further association.

But there is no need to wait for the day when English classes focus on test-taking skills and somehow manage to incorporate Shakespeare into the mix. All a student needs to do is develop the skills necessary to achieve on standardized testing *in addition to* academic excellence in his or her liberal arts curriculum. Then the problems associated with standardized testing resolve, and *Romeo and Juliet* can be the only tragic chapter in a child's experience as student!

Charting the Voyage

Parents and students are discouraged from approaching standardized-testing study materials with nonchalance. Simply put, there is too much at stake and time is not a luxury. The window of opportunity for understanding standardized testing is narrow; the clock does not rewind itself for any student. Prudence and diligence are key; in many cases, sooner really is better than later.

Years ago, many of us unwittingly shared in the standardized testing experience as high school students. But in today's competitive college admissions process, college testing has become far too critical to treat lightly. The fact is that standardized testing results are a great opportunity to compete for scholarship money and acceptance into some of the best universities. Therefore, Standardized testing is far too important to be overlooked or treated as nothing more than *par for the course.* Standardized tests should not be taken *just to see how it goes.* It is ultimately advisable to approach standardized testing with a great deal of energy and solid preparation.

Robert Pimentel & Mateo Pimentel

Staying on Course

For one reason or another, tools largely go unnoticed in our lives. They are fairly underrated and so are the skills needed to wield them. Tools often are associated with jobs that society does not glorify. Yet, similar tools exist in today's classroom: reading tools, math tools, spelling and writing tools, etc. Tools are available to students every day. Even though a student comes into direct contact with these implements, proficiency in the skills necessary to correctly use them is sometimes non-existent or inconsistent. Whatever the case may be, tools are necessary and so are the skills required to capitalize on them.

The problem with underestimating the importance of tools, and developing the skills required to use them, may be accidental. Then again, it may not. Any misgivings associated with tools and the like may, in fact, be attributable to

12

ordinary school assignments, especially ones that require profound memorization. This is where school skills vs. test-taking strategies collide. In standardized testing performance, memorization is equivalent to opening an exorbitant amount of screens on a computer; the microprocessor slows down, unable to efficiently process tasks. By opening fewer screens, processing information becomes more efficient.

Students' brains are bogged down in a similar fashion. Memorizing replaces their profound ability to think critically; thus their capabilities to perform on standardized testing also diminish. Thinking critically is ultimately irreplaceable when seeking excellent standardized testing performance, especially with a powerful gimmick like memorization.

None of this indicates that school assignments are inherently bad. The presumed culmination of school assignments is that they reinforce extremely valuable lessons from the age-old pantheon of liberal arts curricula that have helped humanity's progression over the centuries. Still, as far as standardized testing goes, a key attribute a student must develop is the ability to *not* memorize information; in its stead, students must use tools and skills required for success.

For example, why read a test passage to

memorize the events or details therein when there is obvious access to the information right before a student's eyes? Why go to all that trouble? There is no need. In a reading passage on a standardized exam, the student's ability to assemble clues based on the vocabulary and sentence structure makes the principal, unwavering difference between choosing a correct answer over an incorrect one. It goes without saying; there are many more incorrect answers than correct ones on most standardized tests.

Reaching Safe Harbor

Why is it important for parents to revisit and understand the student experience with standardized testing? Will the knowledge about a few specific questions, coupled with a high degree of proficiency with test taking skills, ensure that their child will perform to the fullest degree? We are positive that the answer is "yes." Parents face a situation where their students are at a loss for resources. After all, students are proficient in school, not necessarily in acing standardized tests. So, how can a student pass or excel on standardized testing when most only score the average? And how can students do well when taking the test without practice? Subpar performance, then, seems a natural spoke in the wheel of this vicious, misunderstood cycle.

Whatever the case may be, there is hope. Parents can assure their students that there is no need to take standardized testing cold and unprepared. Parents can instruct their student that this type of testing requires certain tools, not necessarily taught in school, in order to excel. Parents can then help their student study and prepare adequately, whether that means private instruction or individual study. The student will realize there is no need to omit preparation, no need to resort to tricks like memorization, and no need to only expect average outcomes. Finally, students will test with lifted spirits, knowing that achieving to their maximum potential is more a matter of choice than luck. Yes. There is hope.

THE FOUR FACTORS

I. The Test

One reason why many students perceive their performance on standardized testing as subpar is because they take the test but have no specific training. They take these tests under the assumption that school alone wholly prepares them for the tests. This can be a mistaken assumption. Nevertheless, there is additional training available to help them reach their fullest potential.

In a similar fashion, a substantial amount of parents claim, "My child does not do well on standardized tests." They reach a conclusion based on the scores reported to them from standardized testing evaluations, which include benchmarking students with pretests. Although this may be an accurate statement about a child's performance, and even if a parent has undeniable proof that her child performs poorly on most standardized tests, it does not necessarily follow that the child is a poor test taker, or that he or she is unable to perform well on standardized testing. Again, test preparation and specific tools can absolutely alter the outcome of standardized test scores.

Poor test scores sometimes signify nothing at all. This possibility is especially important for parents to remember. It would be unfair to assign someone the task of baking a cake without providing the recipe. For that matter, you would not ask this of someone who has only eaten cake but never baked one. This is analogous to asking a student to perform well without a recipe for success on standardized testing. The outcome may be subpar, or an inaccurate measure of a child's true ability. But what sort of cake can one really expect to come out of the oven without the discipline of practice and the instructive aid of a recipe?

Consider the following: standardized testing gets away with calling itself 'standard' merely by engineering arbitrary tests. After all, does the standardized test account for the disparity in educational resources that may exist in a state's rural, suburban and inner city setting? This factor also buoys the arbitrariness of the test. If parents invest in a practice guide or study book for standardized testing, they are likely to find a disclaimer that states standardized testing is not an accurate measure of a student's comprehension of subjects, but a measure of how well a student performs on standardized testing.

What does this mean? Well, it means that the type of learning your child does all year long and for countless years before does not necessarily prepare him or her to do well on a standardized test. Absolutely, students of logic are quick to discover the fallacy behind this thinking: simply because the composite pieces of an airplane—nuts bolts, hoses, rubber, etc.—are each respectively light, it does not mean that the entire airplane is light. The same is true for your child and standardized testing performance. Simply because a student takes tests for years, it does not necessarily follow that he or she will perform the same way with standardized testing as with school tests. Even if we argued that a school test is a test, and that the SAT® (Scholastic Aptitude Test)* is a test, we would not properly conclude that your child has experienced standardized testing simply for having taken all sorts of tests at school. The two species of tests are very different.

Another example might help illuminate the fact that standardized testing is not the same as school tests. Consider that English courses use

* SAT is a trademark of the College Board, which does not sponsor or endorse this book.

books and poems, essays, etc., to instruct students in the literary techniques and devices necessary to ascertain what culture deems to be good books or good art. This does not mean that a student, when reaching a point of comprehension of literary techniques/devices, will automatically be able to write the next *New York Times* bestseller. Yet, even though school does not translate to a given readiness for standardized testing, this is not to say that preparing for a standardized test is a substitute for the learning that goes on in school. Students will need to employ the critical thinking they cultivate at school on standardized testing. Truly, it is hard to imagine a replacement for a liberal arts education and all the treasure it holds in store for a student.

Included in the aforementioned struggle is the fact that algebra students will have a teacher instruct them on the material in a chapter by way of lecturing, assigning homework and then testing their mastery of the instructed material. So, is it fair to expect that students should submit to standardized testing unprepared and without instruction? This is all to say that by sending your child to school, you are not guaranteeing them a fair or certain outcome on a standardized test score. In fact, standardized testing is so arbitrary, so removed from subject mastery in school, that students who attend some of the nation's top-ranking schools take the same test as do students of the most underprivileged schools. If it is nearly impossible to identify what schools share in common with one another, then there is no need to expect standardized testing to accurately measure subject mastery nationwide. It is a matter of test *performance*, not necessarily learning.

After realizing that an arbitrary test counts heavily for college admittance and that schooling has basically nothing to do with it, many parents inquire, "Why do some students do well and get perfect scores while my child does less than average (or, about average)?" Again, it is a completely arbitrary test.

There have to be perfect scores possible so as to say that if one student can do it, then they all can. Even though this is also entirely illogical, this functions as a self-serving rationale to explain why some kids do better than others. It often takes the form of the following remark: "Oh, that kid is just smarter than my kid." Even if this were the case, why are they being asked to take the same test?

2. School

It is common for students to design ways in which to pass tests. In fact, children are so smart and open to the world that even though they do not register every detail of a lesson, they will persevere when it comes time for testing at school. Does this mean students will ace tests without really studying or understanding the most elegant nuances of new concepts? No. Nevertheless, the human brain is an incredibly powerful organ, and every child is equipped with one. We have proof of the intelligence inherent in a great number of students, especially in the simple but common situations where students manage to do what is necessary to achieve passing grades or test scores without stellar comprehension. Unfortunately, this presents a problem for excelling with standardized testing.

Students want to perform the work required to excel on standardized testing with the same programming they utilize for schoolwork. That is, students want to rely on things like memorization—capturing finite data from finite chapters and then regurgitating said information on a test to prove mastery. Understandably, students resort to tricks and tendencies that offset the difficulty of schoolwork when full comprehension is lacking. But because they do not otherwise prepare for standardized testing, what may be a useful skill for surviving a unit test in algebra will not suffice when taking a standardized test that requires critical thinking and logical sleuthing.

The fact that students need to prepare for standardized testing with practice and tools becomes even more apparent when students submit to standardized testing with the tools that allow them to excel. Another hang-up may be that students have also become ferocious note-takers. Ask any student why he or she takes such copious notes during a lecture. They may say it is proof that they are learning, or that they think it helps them. Then again, they may not respond at all, because they do not really know why.

One possible truth is that students think if they scribe every word the instructor says, then they will be able to teach themselves at home later when they begin their homework. If such a reason, or one like it, is the case, then they place the burden of teaching on themselves. Instead, they should be as present to the lecture as possible.

Memorizing and learning are not the same things. Thus the problem of trying to remember all words, lessons and things becomes pervasive and overwhelming; it does not necessarily culminate in demonstrating academic prowess on a standardized test. In fact, children are sent to school for many reasons, but ultimately, parents want their children, their students, to learn from great teachers. That is the expectation. Through human interaction in the classroom, and especially with teachers, students develop the tools and capacities they will need to be well formed, thinking human beings. Standardized testing does not score them on this. Therefore, everyday school efforts are not adequate for the majority of students to triumph on standardized tests, which do not require memorizing anything from school.

3. Reading

A good number of students express little interest in reading. They may lack a proficiency of vocabulary that perhaps only comes to most learners after years of reading. This, however, is not to sound the alarm because your child does not need to have a Ph.D. in English to perform well on standardized testing. In broaching the natural deficiencies in a child's progress in reading comprehension, we mean to say that they are still students; learning is a journey, not a destination. Understandably so, they have to be allowed and encouraged to learn, encouraged to read, and to develop a proficiency in and love of vocabulary. Students need time to grow into strong readers. Students need time to be students.

If a child is not strong in reading, does it matter that they are weak readers insofar as standardized testing goes? Well, standardized testing is heavily reading-based and probably for this reason. Test makers know that children are taught that they will receive points on homework and tests at school for deriving the right answer. Still, if students are critically weak in examining the prose of a question, that is, if they cannot understand the question being asked, then the likelihood of a test comprised of arbitrary questions naturally reduces the objective "fairness" of standardized testing. As a result, an overwhelming number of students never go further than the average, *beyond standard.*

4. Money

The creators and vendors of standardized tests have wants, too. Arguably, these are important to consider when digesting this entire process. Most importantly, we need to explore this question: Why do the creators of standardized tests want schools and their curricula to adhere to a blanket list of standards on a national level?

As you may have already surmised, the answer is simple. Given the diversity of cultures and subjects taught across America, and that they have little to do with standardized tests, such diversity poses one of the greatest threats to the future of standardized testing and its profits. Again, one standardized test cannot possibly gauge what every American student studies in high school. Therefore, in order to make the test universally applicable, the test does not accurately reflect what children learn in school.

A parent may rightfully ask, "Why does my child need to suffer through standardized testing if colleges can already evaluate how hard he or she works at school by seeing his or her grades, recommendations, etc.?" The answer is found in the fact that standardized testing serves a powerful master: profit motive. We can assume that test makers and vendors are selling students, who can ace the test, a way in which they can jockey for rewards such as acceptance into the college of their choice or scholarship money.

Students will leave college with a lot of human capital (the investment in an education that increases their skills as workers), which the economy requires to keep itself moving forward. Those who do not earn much scholarship money may incur great debt. Because college graduates can be competitive boosts for the economy as a whole, debt is also part of their motive for working. Thus, the vicious cycle continues and the truth remains clear: it is *imperative* for students to prepare and to do well on standardized testing.

In conclusion, children all across America will experience standardized testing for reasons where the sum is much bigger than the parts. Standardized testing also makes it easy for colleges to arbitrarily divvy up scholarship money and truncate application lists based on scores while avoiding the task of redefining what "merit" looks like on a resume. Students will have varied experiences with standardized testing, experiences as diverse as their academic backgrounds. These experiences fall right in line with the arbitrary nature of the test.

.

HOPE

Good news! With everything we are saying, we do not suggest protesting or keeping students from taking standardized tests; rather, knowing the simple truth behind standardized testing can prove very beneficial. It may even portend scholarship money. If parents know what *really* propels this monster of all testing genres, they know that exploiting such tests by doing well can help a child carve out a path to college admittance, scholarships and even full rides to the school of their dreams.

Working with students for high school placement tests has shown that because students tend not to be practiced, disciplined and critical readers by the time they enter high school, training is absolutely necessary to supplement any normal deficit. Perhaps your child goes to batting practice, piano lessons, algebra tutoring, and summer camp to refine his or her ability to excel in such areas. Likewise, if most students can expect to find themselves at a natural and understandable disadvantage when it comes to test question comprehension (reading), then training is also necessary for them to excel.

Academic training for standardized testing outside of school nearly becomes taboo. Nevertheless, that is precisely where parents are likely to find it. For this reason alone, tests and quizzes given in class may be closer to actually depicting how learning is progressing; however, if standardized testing is as different from school as algebra is from recess, then the only way to address this portion of the student journey is to properly practice and prepare.

If a child performs better with training than without, the training not only warrants time, but becomes essential to a child's success. Even in primary grades, accomplishment with standardized testing may not always translate to future success. If and when children no longer maintain their tendency toward excellence on standardized testing, then understanding what has changed is vital.

Ultimately, the solution is simple: practice and training.

THOUGHTS ON THE CROSSING

Parents know that school is a source of both highs and lows for a child. After all, most parents can recall being a student in their own right. They remember their own hardships and joys as a student; they have "been around the block," as the saying goes. Beyond firsthand experience with student life, parents know just how important it is for a child to receive support in everything. Thus, parents make truly incredible, unselfish sacrifices to be a source of support for their student. As far as school goes, parents count for a lot in the formation of a child. Ultimately, it is only natural for parents to want to help their child succeed. Helping your child train for standardized testing should very much be a part of this process.

Parents share in everything with their child. This especially means school. The shining moments in a child's life are exciting for parents, and the lows can also be fairly unsettling. Yet because a good number of parents spend many years and much energy raising a child, they know all too well that when suffering, the age of the child does not matter. A crying high school student, for example, can be just as disconcerting to a parent as a tearful fourth grader. True, the response to the situation may vary due to age. Nevertheless, parental love and involvement are always present, always there at any turn. At every age, the child is cared for with full attention and a deep love. This is parental dedication.

Parents have a great deal of love for their child. So the fact that parents do not want to see their child suffer makes quite a bit of sense. This love drives parents to find the best ways in which to help their child succeed and how best to support their child.

Each child is unique and responds to parental support in unique ways. Parents know this. They know they have to adapt to the changes in their student's life to continue giving the best type of support possible. They are there to support, love and encourage their child. They are invested in his or her immediate and long-term success. Ultimately, parents are committed and willing to experience the good times as well as the bad.

We can agree once more that as school directly affects the child, so too does it affect the parent. In a very real sense, parents get to experience school all over again. In fact, some parents get to stay in school for a very long time! With each child who passes through the years of schooling required before college admittance, parents learn and re-learn how best to accompany their child. Parents learn how to help ensure their child's success, even if there is no recipe to follow that absolutely guarantees a child's school day will bubble with joy. Parents are so dedicated that they stand by their child even though there is no way to ensure the ideal school experience.

Parents do their best to give a child all the tools necessary for success and happiness. Sometimes, these are very costly efforts. Despite all efforts and all the love in the world, there always exist the variables that can change the course of your child's academic future.

Culturally speaking, there seems a tendency to treat these variables, or intangibles, as unalterable and beyond individual control. Yet, because parents cede what power they have over these variables, they can and often do amount to what seem like either epic successes or catastrophic let-downs for their child. There is good news, however, about one of the most important unknowns affecting your child's life in a very direct way. You know this particular variable by the name of *standardized testing*, and it is well within your control to create the foundation for the best possible outcome for your student, your child.

Notes

Notes

Made in the USA
Middletown, DE
01 June 2021